ARTISTRY
in
AVIAN ABODES

THE LITTLE BIRDHOUSE BOOK

by Dorothy Fitzcharles Weber

Dorothy F. Weber

A Pot Pourri of facts, fun and fancy

D1244735

Illustrations by Helen Jackson Parker

Our special appreciation to:
James Babbitt, Harley Beck, Naomi and Gene Criner,
Sarah Gunn, Elena Lamb, Emily McCardle, Patricia McDonald,
Donald Parker, Winston Spurgeon, Maynard Weber,
Joy Weber, Buddy Wyatt.

A Back Porch Book for Fun and Thoughtful Reading

For my grandchildren:

Kim

Jamie

Matthew

Tim

Kelly

with whom I have made birchbark sandwiches with buttercup fillings served with moss tea at "Indian Rock" beside "our" lake in Maine.

We have tramped and tiptoed over and under "our troll bridge" and searched out duck eggs and hidden nests while feeding the ducks on the pond in Williamsburg.

Now that they are grown may they adopt this little poem as their guiding motto for living.

> "If I can ease one life the aching
> Or cool one pain
> Or help one fainting robin
> Unto his nest again
> I shall not live in vain."
> *Emily Dickinson (circa 1864)*

and to my husband, Mo who adopted this philosophy at an early age.

Why Birdhouses?

"Nature and man's hand must go together."
Jens Jensen

This book is for everyone who loves history, architecture, miniature houses, unusual buildings, folk art, trained art and last but not least, birds, their habits and garden allure.

Birdhouses are an invitation to songbirds to decorate and enliven our gardens, at the same time they help sustain nature's ecological balance with insects.

Here is an opportunity to view and appreciate one of America's oldest conservation themes as started by our native American Indians and overseas ancestors centuries ago.

Threads of history, art, and artistry have been woven throughout the pictures in this little book as a bird would weave its various found materials to create its special nesting place.

The pictures range from many areas of the United States and each abode is uniquely handcrafted.

Single Family Homes

Excluding martin houses, birdhouses are single family one room homes whether a castle or simple cottage.

Porch railings on houses confine the baby birds to their home longer and help keep them from tumbling before they are ready to take wing.

The entrance hole of the birdhouse determines the size bird that can enter and the position of the hole attracts either deep or shallow cavity nesters.

"Hearts and Flowers"

In a beautiful rural area of central Tennessee live a husband and wife folk art team.

They are by name, Cary and Janice Bills and creating folk art in their home is their full time occupation.

During the last two years they have designed and created charming birdhouses for use and for interior decoration.

Their birdhouses are available from New York to Texas in quality shops.

They have been featured in the "Louisville Sunday Journal," "House Beautiful" magazine and have been selected by Disney World and the Museum of American Folk Art for viewing and purchase.

Cary and Janice Bills reside in Belfast, Tennessee.

A reminder of the old favorite song, "Little Church in the Wildwood"

This basket birdhouse is an exemplarly example of Tennessee where baskets have been woven for necessity and pleasure since pioneer days.

Perhaps the basket weaver lived in a home like this one.

A
Comparison
of
Three Artists

At the end of World War I, 1917, a now well recognized, truly American artist, Grant Wood was making doll-sized miniature houses with sponge trees, thatched roofs of straw and twine, paper hollyhocks, mowed and neglected lawns and figures in work clothes.

Many of these could be folded into jack-in-the-box style arrangements and collapsible boxes.

They were all created for Henry S. Ely to promote postwar real estate in the Cedar Rapids, Iowa area.

Grant Wood was also a very talented stained glass artist before he finally was recognized for his uniquely American rural and sometimes satirical oil paintings.

In the spring of 1941 he painted "Spring in Town". There were nine figures, trees, flowers, lawn mowing around quaintly constructed houses, spring repairs, spring cleaning and a myriad of other typical spring activitites. Each part was created from a separate drawing. Very prominent amid all of this activity was a true sign of spring; a birdhouse just like the one he had installed in his early life in Kenwood where he had lived in a tarpaper covered shack in the woods on the outskirts of Cedar Rapids.

Cary and Janice Bills, mentioned on the previous page, have combined a miniature building with real stained glass windows to form a church.

The birds that move into this home will certainly see the surrounding world through "rose colored glasses".

Our next artist also works with stained glass and miniature houses.

"Southern Comfort"

Randy Sewell of Atlanta, Georgia shows a delightful southern humor in his Audubon approved unique avian abodes.

He is a stained glass artist, by profession, but derives real pleasure from his folk created miniature buildings; each equipped with the appropriate accoutrements.

For example, his tarpaper fishing shack has blue wooden waves and alligators, ''swimming'' on springs underneath it. Notice the good luck horseshoe over the front door.

Randy captures true country south in his, Foot Long Hot Dog Stand".

Randy feels that his houses should definitely be put to use out of doors. Only after exposure do the paints and materials mellow.

Randy has exhibited his houses in a variety of shows and the reactions of the viewers have been most enthusiastic.

He has shown in Southeastern Center for Contemporary Art in Winston-Salem, North Carolina among others, Charlotte and Greensboro, North Carolina, also Atlanta, Georgia and as far away from his area as Cambridge, Massachusetts.

His "Diner" will bring back memories for many of us and it is still a common sight in small cities, "on the edge of town".

"Adobe Pottery Shed"

If you long for a taste of the southwest these will make you feel ready for your boots and turquoise and sterling silver concho belt.

"Chili Bowl"

"Cape Hatteras Lighthouse"

An excellent replica of Cape Hatteras, North Carolina historic lighthouse is perfect for those birds who prefer to nest in a deep cavity. It is constructed of fiberglass, sand, rocks, metal and has an antique paint finish. It is twenty one inches high and ten inches wide.

The tallest brick lighthouse in existence is Cape Hatteras Lighthouse on the outer banks of North Carolina. It has been warning ships at sea of the great Diamond Shoal since 1870.

The Diamond Shoal is ten miles off shore and has been named the ''Grave-yard of the Atlantic''.

This sandbar has caused the wreckage of over six hundred ships since the beginning of record keeping.

The historic lighthouse is in danger of being washed away due to shifting sands.

There has been a proposal to lift it and with the aid of rollers move it twenty eight hundred feet to the southwest.

Many people are afraid it could not withstand this serious move. A proposal to use synthetic seaweed to fend off the sea is a recent alternate suggestion.

"Citicorp Center"

After finally getting a vacation from the tumultuous existence of working at the Citicorp Center in New York . . . and you are traveling the highways from New York to Florida look in on one of the numerous factory outlets that dot the byways. This is the way of the 80's.

Be certain to look up Randy Sewell's studio as you are "marching through Georgia". It is located at 38 Muscogee Avenue in Atlanta.

"Loco Joe's"

BIRD BOTTLES
(Hopefully for a bluebird)

A clay bird bottle on a Colonial Williamsburg home is seeing lots of use. They are still made locally of the area clay, turned on a potter's wheel and made waterproof with a clear glaze.

Archaeologists discovered shards of pottery bird bottles in their excavations for preparation of the restoration of Colonial Williamsburg, Virginia.

The first was unearthed on the James Geddy Silversmith property on the Duke of Gloucester Street in the colonial capital.

An early inventory lists a number of bird bottles belonging to a John Burdett in the year 1746.

This is further proof that song birds have delighted humans throughout the centuries.

It has been written that folks in the London slums of White Chapel had wrought iron bird cages attached to their outside walls so that they could enjoy the birds' melodious songs in an otherwise bleak existence.

Providing housing in our gardens is one way of assuring ourselves of the beauty of their songs and fluttering wings.

As you can see the birds are willing to nest close to humans and lots of visitor activity.

"The bluebird carries the sky on his back" Thoreau, and *"Earth on his breast"* John Burroughs.

Pollination, insect control and seed dispersal are other added bonuses.

Bluebirds need much encouragement since they are running out of available nesting spots.

They nest early and often have two broods a year. Bluebird houses should be positioned from four feet to seven feet from the ground.

They work best in open areas and it is possible to have a nesting pair on every acre of open land.

The Pilgrims at Plymouth Colony became enchanted with bluebirds and named them blue robins. They were unfamiliar with them because the bluebird lives only in North America.

"A COPPER BEECH HOUSE"

A "Copper Beech House for Bluebird" is a charming play on words. Its roof of oxodized copper was painstakingly handcut to form leaves by architect Frances Halsband of New York City.

She, with her husband, architect Robert Kliment designed this birdhouse for the 1987 Parrish Art Museum show and auction, in Southampton, Long Island, New York.

This husband and wife team are known for their residential architectural work.

Ms. Halsband, who is president of the Architectural League of New York states that the creation of this house "was an architect's dream" and felt it was truly a fun project although her hands were numb from having cut the intricate little copper leaves.

The actual house was built by Morris and Schorr Builders of painted plywood and copper. It is twelve inches high, eighteen inches wide and eighteen inches long.

This evening, Memorial Day, we sat on our screened porch and watched a pair of bluebirds darting from pine tree to pine tree and were completely thrilled to see these sky blue warblers just a half mile from the center of historic Colonial Williamsburg, Virginia.

"BIRD COTTAGE"

This seems to be reminiscent of an Edward Hopper painting and could have just stepped out of "Cobb's Barns". Can you find the minute birdhouse on the large bird-house?

"Bird Cottage" is suitable for chickadees, bluebirds, nuthatches, titmice, and similar sized birds.

Philetus H. Holt III and Robert W. Russell architects with Holt and Morgan Associates of Princeton, New Jersey designed and constructed this replica of an outbuilding located on the site of one of the original summer houses in the village of "East Hampton", Long Island, New York.

It is listed in "East Hampton's Heritage" that the main house was once painted barn red, hence the paint color selection for the exterior wood.

The house was exhibited at the Parrish Art Museum in Southampton, Long Island.

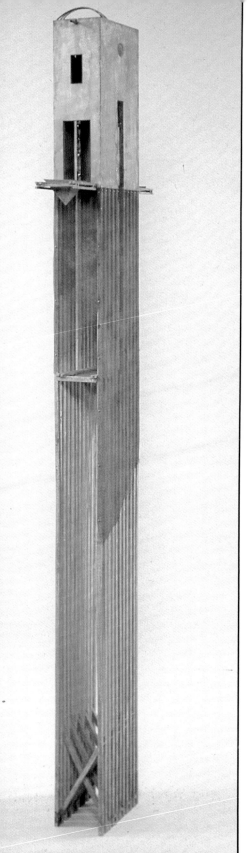

Two of our favorites, members of the thrush family, the robin and blue-bird are provided a deep cavity nesting column.

It is especially appropriate for the bluebird because of his desire for a deep cavity nest but his inability to dig out the cavity for himself.

With urban development we lack open spaces with hollow tree branches and old hollow fence posts.

This house has been designed by Wayne Berg of the architectural firm of Pasanella and Klein and Associates of New York City for the Parrish Art Museum.

It is constructed of patinated copper and wire mesh which should help with thermostatic weather control. The robin's egg blue color is a perfect choice for a bluebird or robin house.

Our bluebirds and robins are of particular concern since Rachel Carson's, "Silent Spring".

THE FROZEN ROBIN
(Anonymous)

See, see what a sweet little prize I have found!
A robin that lies half benumbed on the ground.
Well housed and well fed, in your cage you will sing,
And make our dull winter as gay as the spring.
But stay — sure 'tis cruel, with wings made to soar,
To be shut up in prison, and never fly more;
And I, who so often have longed for a flight,
To keep you a prisoner — would that be right?
No, come pretty robin, I must set you free,
For your whistle, though sweet, would sound
   sadly to me.
(from a book compiled by James Reeves).

This house now calls Atlanta, Georgia home.

It was created by architect, Simon R. Thoresen of Broadway, New York City and his partner Sean Sculley in a collaborative effort with Robinson Iron Company of Alexander City, Alabama.

All the materials were donated and it was a part of the Parrish Art Museum 1987 show and auction.

The post and oakleaf branches made of cast iron support the redwood house as a tree would a nest.

This was to quote Mr. Thoresen ''an enjoyable project'' resulting from ''a happy combination of southern ingenuity and yankee charm''.

Can you find a winged intruder?

Would this house have had appeal for Mark Catesby, J. J. Audubon, or Thomas Bewick for one of their beloved birds? To me, it is a reminder of my son, Jim's Cub Scout project of the 1950's.

Secretly created, touchingly wrapped and proudly presented to his family at holiday time.

It was treasured as it graced a backyard apple tree next to the apple tree containing his personally designed and constructed tree house.

It was an ever present memento of an eight year old boy who even today as a grown man still loves to create with wood.

The little finches nested last season in our hanging Boston fern (the nest is still in it) and their second brood was developed over one of our front porch lights.

The nearly constant singing provided hours of dinner music outside our window.

They had a birds' eye view of us and we a people's eye view of them.

"A Woven Finch House"

"AN IMMIGRANT FROM THE WEST"

The house finch is native to desert brush in Texas, the southwest, and far west.

He made an unusual appearance on the eastern scene. The finches were brought from California in the 1940's to be sold as cagebirds in the New York City area.

When the sellers found this was illegal they turned them loose to fend for themselves and they managed to survive in the city and also on Long Island.

They are now established from Maine to the Carolinas. Their lovely warble is heard while courting and nesting.

Both male and female tend the young. A favorite nesting spot is under an overhang close to people. Perhaps this is a result of New York City survival.

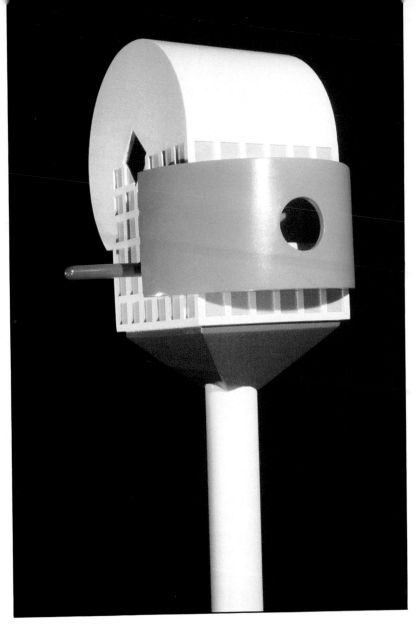

"HOUSE FOR FINCH OR SPARROW"

Contrast this modern architectural creation with the simple woven finch house on page 20.

This was created by the architects of Gwathmey Siegel and Associates of New York City for the Parrish Art Museum show, "Architects Design Birdhouses".

The little house is made of painted wood and epoxy. The actual house measures ten inches by ten inches and stands sixty inches above the ground.

The colors and materials used create an interesting garden ornament and add a definite contrast to greenery.

"SAILING ALONG"

This unusual "House for Finch" was designed by a young residential architect, Ernest G. Schieferstein of Sag Harbor, Long Island, New York.

It was created for the Parrish Art Museum 1987 summer show and charity auction.

The nautical theme is quite evident and aptly so because this part of Long Island has numerous beaches and lovely beach homes.

Mr. Schieferstein told me about its construction and indicated that it was really "fun to do".

The frame is bent aluminum that was sand-blasted for an interesting finish. The aluminum was bent by the cabinetmaker, David Moesell who also did the actual construction.

The wooden box is fashioned from Alaskan Yellow Cedar that is very hardy in the out of doors. The bottom can be opened for cleaning by removing four brass screws.

"House for Finch's" crowning glory is its spinaker sailcloth sail canopied above the little house.

It is now a part of the collection of Reckson and Associates Builders and graces the lobby of the Huntington-Melville Corporate Center.

Cedar logs individually handcrafted for one of a kind birdhouses turned a whim into a fascinating, rewarding and therapeutic recovery from heart surgery for retired army veteran, Ken Dickinson of Williamsburg, Virginia countryside, an area called Norge.

His very first house was built for purple martins. Soon Ken photographed log cabins and houses that he wished to portray.

He knows the dimensions necessary for housing the nests and then he creates with no actual pattern.

The sizes of his houses have ranged from 10 to 42 compartments and some are 24 inches wide, 26 inches tall and 42 inches long.

Ken has probably built in excess of 125 houses, taking from two days to a week to complete.

Your own home may be reproduced in miniature for your feathered friends.

Ken's houses are now found in many areas of the United States. Word of mouth has been his success story.

I first discovered his creations while looking into the backyard of the owner of a favorite bar-b-que establishment. They rose majestically above the fence and could easily be admired from the eaterie's parking lot.

This chalet was inspired by a trip to Austria, the homeland of Ken's wife.

Another veteran used birdhouse building as recovery therapy. This rustic birdhouse was built at a Veteran's Administration Hospital in Dayton, Ohio by Alex Szima and is now treasured by his daughter Madeline German, in Charlotte, North Carolina.

This simply constructed cottage birdhouse is a twin of the real family house it resides beside. They were lovingly painted to match each other and they blend well in their suburban, Capitol Landing Road location in Williamsburg, Virginia. The birdhouse is occupied and the new residents of the main cottage are leaving the birdhouse exactly where it was found; on top of an old tree stump.

THE WREN BUILDING
WILLIAMSBURG, VIRGINIA

The architect's architect Sir Christopher Wren was born in 1632 in England.

He was the inventor of many important (and still in use today) inventions and all executed in his teen years. The sign language for the deaf, a pneumatic machine, and a universal sundial are to his credit.

He studied at Oxford and became an architect following a public appointment to the chair of astronomy professor.

After the great fire of London in 1666 he redesigned the city and supervised much of the building.

His specialty was towers, steeples, and spires. St. Paul's Cathedral is his greatest achievement.

It is believed that the Christopher Wren building at my alma mater was built from his English plans and imported British materials.

Classes are still held today in front of colonial fireplaces at not so comfortable benches and desks in this historic building at the College of William and Mary in Williamsburg, Virginia.

One end of the building contains a lovely chapel in which many weddings have taken place.

The opposite end of the Wren building houses the beautifully paneled Great Hall. It is here that the traditional English Yule Log ceremony takes place for the college students each December with background music of the fine college choir.

"Sir Christopher's Wren House"

This birdhouse, the creation of Michael Graves, architect was designed for the Parrish Art Museum special exhibition in 1987.

Mr. Graves is located in Princeton, New Jersey in the shadows of another renowned colonial college, Princeton University.

He has superbly combined an architecturally famous person with a tiny bird, "the wren" in his interpretation of "Sir Christopher's Wren House".

It was uniquely created from plexiglass and the bronze paint gives the little building a weathered patina.

To learn more about this prominent architect refer to July, 1988 "House and Garden" magazine. An interesting feature article entitled "The Prince of Princeton" appears on pages 132 - 139.

UNINVITED GUESTS?

In the shadow of the Sangre de Christo Mountains of northern New Mexico 7000 feet above sea level Chimayo is located. It is a rural picturesque village on the high road from Santa Fe to Taos.

The village is renowned for its fine weavings and Santuario de Chimayo, its beautiful old church built in 1813 - 1816 while still under Spanish rule.

Its curative mud has attracted those seeking physical and psychological healing for over 150 years.

Discarded crutches, slings and handwritten prayer pleas fill one tiny room.

On Good Friday a pilgrimage takes place to the Sanctuario from near and far.

At the main altar and along the sidewalls one can view some of the finest native folk carved bultas, retablos, santos and handcarved benches.

This could be the American version of Mount Subasio in Italy near Assisi where Saint Francis preached to the birds over 800 years ago as memorialized in a Giotto fresco.

The Santuario and all the surrounding village walls are made of adobe (a sundried sand, straw and mud mixture).

Atop one of these walls are miniature santuarios handcrafted lovingly and primitively by religiously inspired craftsmen of years past.

The area birds have made their own pilgrimages down from the surrounding mountains and call these opened door, opened window miniature churches temporary homes.

They by chance rest at a perfect height above the ground, perhaps the "squatters" are mountain bluebirds.

Chimayo is the Tewa Indian description of the red "flaking" stone that paints the landscape.

The mountain bluebird differs from the eastern bluebird in that he has a white abdomen rather than the rust and his back is the bright blue of the New Mexican sky. The wings are longer and more graceful than his eastern relatives. His flight is more swallowlike as he soars down from the mountains.

"AN ADOBE ABODE"

A clay finch bottle resembling the native adobe hangs in a century old pinon tree in Santa Fe, New Mexico.

The pinon nuts are relished by the area birds as well as gourmet cooks. The tree started to grow at about the same time as Archbishop Lamy arrived in Santa Fe.

He started planting trees in this desert land at his "Villa Pintoresca" made famous in Willa Cather's, "Death comes for the Archbishop".

The "Bishop's Lodge" on the outskirts of Santa Fe is a reminder of him today. His old homestead is visited by the famous and not so famous.

Guests stay in the Inn surrounded by the historic trees that are so valued in this semi-desert land.

MY SINGING BIRD

*(From Folksongs and Ballads Popular in Ireland
collected by John Loesberg)*

I have seen the lark soar high at morn
to sing up in the blue,
I have heard the black-bird pipe its song,
the thrush and the linnet too.
But none of them can sing so sweet, my singing
bird as you, Aah . . . . . .
My singing bird as you.

If I could lure my singing bird from its own
cozy nest,
If I could catch my singing bird, I would warm it on
my breast.
And on my heart my singing bird would sing bird
would sing itself to rest,
Aah . . . . . .
would sing itself to rest.

Whimsical Birdhouses
by Randy Sewell

"Drive-In"

"Blimp Hanger"

"Crazy Eddies"

"Water Tower"

"Oasis"

"Muffler House"

"OKLAHOMA OKAY"

Woolaroc Museum in Bartlesville, Oklahoma derives its name from (Woo)ds, La(kes), and (Roc)ks.

It is composed of many things: a wildlife preserve, a lodge, and is national Y — Indian Center (part of the national Y.M.C.A).

The Phillips family of petroleum fame were its founders and benefactors. It operates today as a philanthropic and charitable non-profit organization.

Some of the finest southwestern art is on display here. Remington, Russell, and Joe Beeler bronzes are scattered among Indian artifacts.

There are five main galleries in the museum and an upper and lower level.

Archaeological finds in Oklahoma, the culture of southwestern Indians, such as the Pueblos, Navajos, and Apaches along with excellent pottery and basket collections are displayed in two of the rooms.

The plains Indians of Oklahoma, Cowboys, and Outlaws of the west comprise the collections in the third and fourth galleries.

The fifth room is an excellent portrayal of history as seen through the art works of contemporary artists: Harry Jackson and Ernest Berke, to mention two.

The Johnstone and Keeler store — where some of the grain was traded and sold.

The local mill — where grains were ground.

The out-of-doors area holds a special exhibition for those interested in birdhouses and history.

Curtis Sydebotham, a museum employee has created replicas of many of the areas historic buildings, incorporating them into his inhabited birdhouses.

These birdhouses have been a tradition at Woolaroc for as long as the museum folks can remember.

Searles Grant, a master carpenter was in charge of them for many years and eventually he taught his stepson, Curtis the upkeep and manner of construction so that both men have added interesting new designs over the years.

Curtis may be reached at the museum on Route 3, Bartlesville, Oklahoma if one wishes to learn more about these handsome historic monuments.

A county jail — now housing "outlaw" birds.

An Oklahoma apartment house.

Renowned folk artist, Nancy Thomas lives and works in historic York-town, Virginia.

Her whimsical angels, animals and buildings are in many private and public collections.

The Reagan's White House Christmas tree has been adorned with her wooden ornaments.

The movie, "Tootsie" starring Dustin Hoffman displayed her folk art in a New York apartment scene.

Just looking at her work produces a happy warm feeling to the viewer.

The Yorktown Birdhouse series combines history with conservation and of course, artistry.

Nancy's birdhouses are in gardens throughout the United States and Canada. Many are in prominent citizens' collections and on occasion a "birth announcement" will arrive at Nancy's folk art shop announcing the birth of baby Martins, baby Wrens, baby Buntings, and little baby Robin. (Think how many names of birds are associated with humans).

Actually helping our wild birds, creating beauty, promoting American history are something that Nancy should be very proud of accomplishing.

This little church birdhouse is Nancy's interpretation of historic Grace Episcopal Church situated in Yorktown, Virginia on a hill overlooking the York River.

This was the site of the surrender of Lord Cornwallis, the British officer, at the final land and water battle of the American Revolution.

The church was built in 1697 and was 84 years old October 19, 1781 when it witnessed this historic surrender.

Interestingly, Lt. Jean Audubon, commander of the "Queen Charlotte" corvette (a French ship) anchored in the York River witnessed this world changing surrender also.

Lt. Audubon's superior was Admiral the Comte de Grasse.

Lt. Jean Audubon's fame today is his renowned son, John James Audubon, our nationally loved naturalist and bird artist.

"Grace Episcopal Church Birdhouse".

"THE MOORE HOUSE BIRDHOUSE"

Nancy also makes the historic Moore House birdhouse which actually is on the old Temple Farm near Yorktown.

This house is the true scene of the finalization of Cornwallis' surrender to General George Washington.

It is a national landmark owned by the United States Government. The Temple Farm was named for the occupant from 1660-1686, the Reverend Peter Temple.

At the time of the 1834 purchase of the farm by Sheldon Shield within a a ruined circular wall a heap of tombstones was uncovered and most interestingly one bore the name of Colonial Virginia Governor Spottswood.

Augustine Moore who purchased the farm earlier in 1769 was the grandson of Governor Spottswood.

"A COTTAGE INDUSTRY"

Lady Slipper Designs of Bemidji, Minnesota in the northern woods and Indian wild rice country is the home of a flourishing cottage industry.

Since 1973, as part of the Northwest Economic Development, it has helped provide income for hundreds of artisans and their families in an otherwise economically depressed area.

The unusual houses are designed by Fern Letnes and Henry Baker and have the approval of naturalists and ornithologists.

Each house is individually handcrafted of Minnesota kiln-dried pine. They can easily be cleaned and pole mounted.

The houses are snow white and represent miniature mission churches, Greek Revival architecture, Victorian and saltbox styles and a very traditional church resembling New England village churches.

Group Housing for Colonies of Birds

WHY DO BIRDS LIVE IN COLONIES?

Researchers are finding that they may tell each other where they have discovered food.

The many bird traits that have been thought to be instinctive are more apt to be learned from each other by demonstration.

Crows and jays are considered very smart and are clever enough to warn others of approaching danger.

Unfortunately the old fashioned scare crow is seldom a threat to jays and crows.

I have read of a crow that could peel the cap off of a milk bottle and drink the milk between the milkman's deliveries.

There is a story about crows that could reel in fishing lines to enjoy the fishermen's catches in their absence.

"HOME GROWN HOUSES"

Native American Indians provided the very first martin housing. The gourds they grew were hollowed out, hung in groups from trees where they dried naturally.

Audubon observed that the martins taking over the gourds were so audacious that they chased away vultures attracted to the Indians' vension.

A purple martin eats over 2000 mosquitoes every day. What a truly natural bug light!

Gourds must be cleaned, varnished or painted with water-base paint at the end of each season and stored for preservation while the martins are on winter vacation in South America then brought out and hung by April for their return north.

You may order prepared gourds of many sizes for a variety of birds from "Home Grown Houses", Recreational Specialists on Route 2 in Falling Waters, West Virginia.

The Leatherman family who operate "Home Grown Houses" have had purple martins come each year for a long time and they have discovered their preference for gourds.

They have been growing their own gourds for some time and realized that wrens and blue-birds love to call a gourd "home".

Lately they have supplied their gourd houses to a national market. Each gourd has a gloss finish and perches are installed in all but the martin houses.

This is a unique business involving three generations of the Leatherman family.

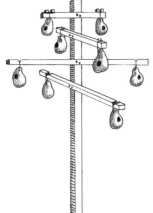

For the Gardener: It could be rewarding if you have a garden and the time and patience to try and create your own Indian martin housing. The following diagram is a good example.

"GARDEN OF THE GODS"
Between Santa Fe and Albuquerque, New Mexico

Birds are our only living holdover from pre-historic times in their original form.

Vertical beds of colorful sandstone and mud-stone of the Galisteo Formation were deposited in streams 70 million years ago.

Originally they were horizontal sheets and have tilted to their present vertical position by mountain building forces beneath the earth's surface.

The indentations in this pre-historic stone have been a natural form of bird colony housing for centuries in the desert area of northern New Mexico. These indentations house rock wrens, canyon wrens and other desert birds.

This and the previous page are both basically colony housing from nature but such a vast difference.

"BUNGALOW BIRD COLONY"

Contrast this grouping with that on the previous page. This was designed by Lee H. Skolnick of Architecture and Design located in New York City.

"Bungalow Bird Colony" was displayed in the May-July 1987 exhibition at Southampton's Parrish Art Museum.

"Better Homes in Garden"
of plexiglass and wood.

MORE ON MARTIN HOUSING

Each opening in a martin house leads to an individual apartment. If kept extremely clean after nesting they will return year after year unless some other tenant has slipped in, such as the ubiquitous sparrow or starling. I have observed in the Virginia countryside martin houses that have been literally sealed over each opening in the winter to assure the martins of spotless spring house-cleaned abodes.

Research verifies that in the city of Greencastle, Pennsylvania a colony of purple martins appeared continuously every year from approximately 1840 to 1978. It is not known why they abandoned Greencastle.

Unfortunately most of the martin houses there have been dismantled. The lady who provided this information from Greencastle was none other than Sarah "Martin".

Griggsville, Illinois now claims to be the "purple martin capital of the world". The Nature Society there has many publications on martin houses and the care of purple martins.

"Almost every country tavern has a martin box on the upper part of its sign-board", Audubon noted, "and I have observed that the handsomer the box the better does the inn generally prove to be".

A COLUMBARIUM

The Dove-Cote or "Columbarium" has its origin in the days of the Roman Empire.

These houses were designed for doves or pigeons. They began as a tower of stone with holes in the walls from floor to ceiling.

As many as 5000 birds could have been quartered in one tower. English gardeners frequently incorporated dove-cotes in their gardens.

Although smaller, the tower shape prevailed. A favorite color was blue gray.

The early English colonists arriving on the American shores brought the dove-cote designs with them from England.

Pigeon or squab was a delicacy served on the 18th century groaning board.

The 18th century garden at the George Wythe House in Colonial Williamsburg, Virginia contains a practical wooden dove-cote, inhabited by free flying pigeons.

The pigeons and doves of Colonial Williamsburg are fortunate indeed. Within a very close area they have access to a variety of abodes.

A practical use for an empty loft in an outbuilding; entrance holes for these birds.

"GARDEN MAGIC"

This adaptation of an English Dove-Cote is the creation of a cottage industry in Colerain, North Carolina. They call themselves "Lazy Hill Cottage Industry".

It is suitable for formal, cottage and contemporary gardens. The roof is cedar shingles harvested by the creators and the walls are made of painted cypress.

I came upon this charming adaptation in a magical new garden shop in Charlotte, North Carolina while on a recent visit to that area.

"Garden Magic" shop is owned and operated by some young ladies who stock all the things you dream of someday gracing your own ornamental grounds.

"Garden Magic", 605 Providence Road
Charlotte, North Carolina

A BRICK PLANTATION DOVE-COTE

Shirley Plantation is still a working plantation along the James River in Charles City County, Virginia.

The Hill Carter family who are living there at the present are the tenth generation of the original Carter family to inhabit the Georgian mansion that was built in the early 18th century.

Perhaps the squab raised in this dove-cote still garnish the family's riverside picnics along with other traditional Tidewater Virginia delicacies.

A CONTEMPORARY DOVE-COTE

There is known to be an interesting design from 1779 for a dove-cote at Monticello, the home of Thomas Jefferson in Charlottesville, Virginia.

A modern day architect, Richard Meier of New York City has created a contemporary dove-cote.

He has achieved national and international acclaim for his designs of buildings, furniture, paintings, collages and architectural drawings.

The High Museum of Art in Atlanta, Georgia is one of his designs, completed in 1983.

He has been commissioned to design the J. Paul Getty Center in Los Angeles, California.

A sixteen story office building in Bridgeport, Connecticut and the new City Hall and Central Library in the Hague, Netherlands are on the drawing board.

He has taught at Cooper Union, Yale and Harvard Universities. A few of his many honors are election to the American Academy, French Government honor as an Officer of Arts and Letters, a member of the International Academy of Architecture, and an Honorary Fellows in the Royal Institute of British Architects.

This Contemporary Dove-Cote was designed by Mr. Meier for the Parrish Art Museum ''Architects Design Birdhouses'' show of fifty some nationally and internationally recognized architects.

This is truly American: Red, White, and Blue.

THE PHEASANT

America's mother country England has already been credited with being the direct forerunner of our colonial dove-cotes.

Thatched roofs dot the English countryside and thatching is far from a lost art.

Each thatcher working today has his own individual symbol made of straw and placed on a rooftop.

While our family lived during the month of April in a 400 year old thatched cottage near Ilminster, Somerset, England amid apple orchards and flocks of sheep we enjoyed watching the birds darting in and out of their ready made straw nests tucked into the edges of the thatching on our roof.

Such beautiful chirpings awakened us each morning. "Sweet is the breath of morn her rising sweet, with charm of earliest birds", John Milton from "Paradise Lost".

Many local rooftops had a straw pheasant atop and hearing of a fine secluded restaurant named "The Pheasant" we kept wondering which thatched cottage was "The Pheasant" since we were told there was no advertising for this house of fine dining.

How humorous to find that none of these were the eatery we wanted and merely the local thatcher's logo for that area.

We finally were directed to the well kept secret, located in Seavington St. Mary it was worth the search — DELICIOUS!

This dove-cote is used for mourning doves. In England a pair of doves is put in the house with food and water, the doors are covered with wire for several days and when the doves are released they are trained to return as long as food and water are provided.

Seven men in Devon, England create these thatched birdhouses from locally grown thatch. It is the same thatch as that used on this type cottage for hundreds of years.

These are available from:
ENGLISH THATCH
909 A. W. 22nd Street
Houston, Texas.

Birds' Nests

"For time will teach thee soon the truth,
There are no birds in last year's nest!"
by Henry Wadsworth Longfellow

THE RED ROBIN
by John Clare (from the book compiled by James Reeves)

Cock Robin, he got a new tippet in spring,
And he sat in a shed and heard other birds sing.
And he whistled a ballad as loud as he could,
And built him a nest of oak leaves by the wood,
And finished it just as the celandine pressed
Like a bright burning blaze, by the edge of its nest,
All glittering with sunshine and beautiful rays,
Like high polished brass, or the fire in a blaze;
Then sung a new song on the edge of the brere;
And so it kept singing the whole of the year.
Till cowslips and wild roses blossomed and died,
The red robin sang by the old spinney side.

In an old history it was mentioned that a delicacy for invalids was "Robin Broth". Fortunately no recipe was given and it would be unacceptable today with our many wildlife protective organizations.

TREES
by Joyce Kilmer

I think that I shall never see
A poem lovely as a tree.
A tree that looks at God all day
And lifts her leafy arms to pray.
A tree that may in summer wear
A nest of robins in her hair.
Poems are made by fools like me,
But only God can make a tree.

BAFFLING BIRDS

Birds have been known to build nests in what we would consider to be very odd places.

It might be a coat pocket, a pocket in a shirt drying on a clothesline, old baskets, hanging plants, flower pots, mailboxes, and even street and traffic lights.

John James Audubon captured this trait of wrens in his 1824 pastel and water-color of baby wrens reaching out of a very old hat toward their mother.

He said, "I hope you will look at the little creatures peeping out to meet their mother, which has just arrived with a spider, whilst the male is on the lookout, to interpose should any intruder come near".

Audubon also is believed to have said, "I knew of one nest in the pocket of an old broken down carriage and many in an old hat."

AUDUBON AND WOOD
BRAQUE, WEBER AND GAUGHIN
(Birds as seen through the eyes of painters)

When John James Audubon was a young boy his room was cluttered with birds' nests, feathers, and eggs.

He developed keen vision at a young age and this along with his awareness contributed immensely to his patience which in turn complemented his art of painting wildlife.

Many years after Audubon, in 1901 in the Anamosa, Iowa "Eureka", weekly newspaper an interesting paragraph appeared:

"Master Grant Wood only ten years of age, reports he has found 55 varieties of birds in this neighborhood (of Iowa). His communication on this subject is very interesting and shows that he is an observing, thoughtful, wide awake boy".

How interesting that a love of and curiosity about birds at an early age has culminated in more than one talented artist.

In reverse, Georges Braque, the French painter created illusionary birds throughout his later years, beginning at about age 57.

One such bird graced a French postage stamp in honor of his eightieth birthday. It was a fifty centime stamp and depicted a lovely white bird on a blue field. Our American equivalent might be our dove of peace.

He painted another bird returning to its nest on the ceiling in the "Louvre" in Paris.

Braque's graceful bluebirds, Pelias and Neleus were used as a jewelry design.

Another twosome of colorful birds appear in isolation on bare tree branches in Max Weber's, "Fleeing Mother and Child" painted in 1913. A third bird is barely seen in distant flight. The simple lines and primitiveness of these birds would also adapt beautifully to jewelry or fabric and tapestry design.

Paul Gaughin, a successful Paris stockbroker left this and his family too, to pursue art, living in a little hut on the island of Tahiti painting exotic birds, plants and natives. Unfortunately he did not live to realize his own success in painting as we recognize him today.

FEATHER YOUR NEST

Birds are always in need of nesting materials. They line their birdhouses even though they have protective walls.

Exceptions are flickers and woodpeckers who should be supplied with sawdust or similar on which to lay and protect their eggs and baby birds.

It is an excellent idea to place six inch (no longer for fear of entanglement) lengths of string or yarn, papers and feathers in the vicinity of a birdhouse or nesting area as encouragement.

The materials can be loosely woven through a piece of openwork fabric and hung prominently to attract the attention of the scavengering nest makers.

Male wrens build dummy nests to offer a choice to the female wren who then disects and rebuilds the one of her choice.

It has been substantiated that a wren's nest in the midwestern part of the United States contained the following:

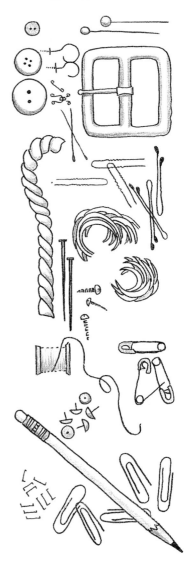

hairpins
large and small nails
tacks
staples
pins
pencil lead
paper clips
safety pins
wires
hooks
buckle

Can you imagine!

Limerick by Edward Lear (1812-1888)
There was an old man with a beard,
Who said, "It is just as I feared!
Two owls and a hen, four larks and a wren
Have all built their nests in my beard".

THE HAIRCUT
(a true story)

Many years ago, as the mother of a little girl with strawberry blond curls I decided it was time for her to have a haircut.

I took her outside the back door and we sat on our patio. It was a lion like day in March and as quickly as I trimmed, the curls were caught by the wind and whisked away to unknown places.

More curls grew back on little Patty's head and curled ever so tightly with the aid of the extreme heat and humidity of the month of August.

As summer progressed accompanied with many rain showers weeds, weeds, and more weeds appeared.

The flower beds were overrun with enemy invaders so the mother and daughter knelt to weed under some low bushes growing by the front of their country home.

A wonderful surprise!
Nestled low in a little evergreen bush was a tiny deserted wren's nest. It appeared to be woven with golden threads.

On closer scrutiny we realized that Patty's curls had come home to rest in the dainty nest and it was treasured for the opening day in September at Woodhill Elementary School to share with fourth grade science class.

Nature has truly fascinating stories to share with us.

THE GOLDEN NECKLACE
(a fanciful story)

An elegant Hungarian china pattern was designed many years ago in Europe for an elegant lady, Mrs. Rothchild of the famous European family.

It is considered to be the one truly hand-painted china available today.

Each artist may paint the designs of birds, butterflies and plants in any pattern he wishes, so no two pieces are exactly alike.

It appears that during the planning stages of selecting designs such as birds and flowers Mrs. Rothchild misplaced her favorite and most precious gold necklace.

A royal search took place and when all hope of retrieving it was lost the gardener discovered it. It had been woven by a bird into its tiny nest.

For evermore the gold necklace will be memorialized on each hand-painted piece of china, probably hidden in a tree branch or dangling from a twig.

THE NEST EGG

While browsing through an antique shop on a recent jaunt I came upon a small oval white milkglass object that stirred immediate vivid recollections of my childhood on "Greentrees Farm" in Pennington, New Jersey in the 1930's.

Although this small white milkglass egg was totally out of context I could feel its smoothness and hold it carefully in my cupped hand and reminisce.

My father seemed to be saying to me, "be very careful and don't drop it or it will break. Put it back in the straw nest because a broody hen will sit on it and it will start laying eggs for hatching".

This seemed miraculous to me as a little girl. Did it help chickens lay brown eggs also or just ones that laid white ones?

It held the same mystique as catching a bird by shaking salt on its tail. Somehow I never managed to catch one with this method and I even used my mother's very best white and gold Lenox salt shaker. (Little did I realize that if I got close enough to put the salt on its tail it would follow that the bird could be easily captured).

Another mystery was the double "yolker" eggs that were sometimes served to us for breakfast. We thought them a real treat but with today's concern with cholesterol perhaps they were not the treat we thought.

This also brings to mind the beauty, stylization, and ability of the artist, Grant Wood to create chickens by making tiny arcs such as half moons or fingernail cuticles to create the Plymouth Rock Hen who I knew so well on the farm. The chicken drawings were first made by Grant with a pencil at the age of three, followed many years later by his famous chicken painting, "Adolescence".

The chicken coop, as seen at the Wythe House, Colonial Williamsburg, Virginia.

BIRD'S NEST SOUP

Can you really eat a bird's nest?

Yes, if it belongs to a relative of the European Swift.

Many years ago in Java a well known plant explorer, David Fairchild, visited caves in southern Java inhabited by swifts.

He and his party descended deeply into the caves, crawling down crude bamboo ladders in order to view these rare nests.

The nests were attached to the rock walls as a chimney swift would do in our country.

The consistency was soft as a mushroom and translucent. The foamy saliva from the swift's salivary glands creates the nest.

Oriental islands and southeastern Asia are the main habitat of these birds.

The difficulty in retrieving the nests and the right to do so created a lucrative business in former years.

AND NOW WOULD YOU LIKE TO TRY SOME?

Bird's Nest Soup
(Yen-wo-t'ang)

1 cup loosely packed dried bird's nest
1 whole chicken breast (approximately 3/4 pound)
1/4 cup cold water
1 teaspoon cornstarch
1 teaspoon salt
2 egg whites
1 quart chicken stock
1/8 teaspoon white pepper
2 tablespoons cornstarch (dissolved in 3 tablespoons
cold chicken stock or water)
an eighth inch thick slice of Smithfield ham, minced
serves 6

Consult a Chinese cookbook for actual preparation procedure. You may order bird's nest fragments from Asian specialty stores.

And now that your mouth is salivating for this delicacy . . . . . .

EL NIDO

Bird's nest soup an ancient and gourmet repast brings to mind a restaurant in an old country house in Tesuque, New Mexico that has taken the Spanish words for "the nest", "El Nido" as its name.

"EL NIDO" is by no means a newcomer to the artists and Indian pueblo area outside Santa Fe countryside.

It has been in business since 1939, almost fifty years. The entryway of this excellent seafood restaurant displays framed shadowboxes of a collection of real birds' nests and eggs on the wall. These are the delightfully eyecatching creation of Ford Ruthling.

JUST FOR FUN

How does the word "NEST" look in other languages?

German — das nestei or das nest

Dutch — verblijf

Swedish — näste

Italian — nido or riparo or covo

Portugese — ninho

Latin — nidus

Polish — gniazdo

Welsh — nyth

Norwegian — rede or hekke

Hungarian — feszek

French — nid

RACHEL — THE AMISH TEACHER
(a modern true story)

Once upon a time there lived a young Amish girl. Her name was Rachel. She taught school in a one room Amish schoolhouse across the road from her Delaware farm.

Rachel wove beauty and enchantment into her school lessons by using her birds' nest collection.

They personified the simplicity and sincerity of her heritage. Through these nature made teaching aids basic principles of science, religion and appreciation of nature's miracles could help prepare her pupils for their agrarian paths down the road of life.

My first meeting with Rachel was in her quilt shop after she had retired from teaching.

The simplicity of her many nests adorning the nooks and crannies of her sunporch shop were as naively appealing as a Rousseau painting.

This is an artist's drawing made from a red eyed vireo's nest. It was a gift from Rachel to my daughter.

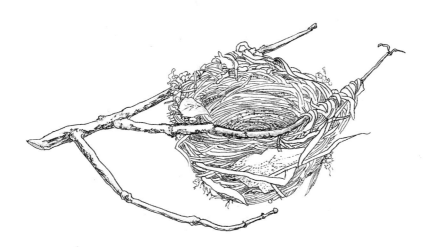

A red eyed vireo always weaves a cup of plant fibers mixed with strips of bark, then trims the nest with lichen and fastens it to a forked twig.

"And hark how blithe the Throstle sings, He too is no mean preacher;
Come forth into the light of things, Let Nature be your teacher".
by William Wordsworth

AN EDUCATED BIRD

Teaching in a private kindergarten before the Commonwealth of Virginia established public kindergartens subjected me to mostly very happy situations, however on occasion a nerve jolting happening could suddenly surface.

Such was the spring morning in May at about 8.00 a.m. when I arrived at the little house where I taught in one small room with an adjacent lavatory, an "in between room", another kindergarten room and a kitchen.

The classroom appeared somewhat stuffy so I hastened to raise all four windows to allow some delightful breezes and sunshine to enter our screenless portals.

What to my wondering eyes should appear but a miniature flying object that entered by the southeastern exposure and chirped and circled, chirped and circled the room perching on one table after another and making herself very much at home observing the children's spring drawings of birds and finally settling on an alphabet book.

Looking at the clock I realized that at any moment my happy-faced youngsters would appear.

WHAT TO DO?

Miss A. B. Seedy (a good name for a bird in school) decided to investigate the tiny lavatory whose door stood open. Snap decision! I closed the door leaving Miss A. B. Seedy imprisoned.

Just in time! The children began to straggle in, placing their snack bags in the cupboard and the girls placed their chapel caps on their heads.

I quickly penned a note to the principal hoping that our Miss A. B. Seedy could be released to the great out of doors while we were in the sanctuary.

The note was securely folded and given with instructions to one of the more reliable children to take to the office and then meet us in the chapel.

Chapel service, by chance was woven around the beauties of spring, birds, flowers, new life and joy.

We returned to our little room, settled down and a young lad went to open the lavatory door for a visit.

Out flew Miss A. B. Seedy and hilarity, commotion and downright pandemonium broke loose.

Robin, my messenger had not been able to intercept the principal before she left for chapel service so Miss A. B. Seedy was more ready than ever to test her wings after her confinement.

After a number of low zooming circles she exited by way of her entrance and disappeared in the lush green foliage of a nearby crepe myrtle tree.

We had the wonderful privilege of observing her raise three baby sparrows in a little nest in a low hanging branch in that very same tree.

She was so fond of us that we could actually peer into her snug little nest.

It's amazing what a little education will do toward understanding of others.

This little (bird) house resembles our little kindergarten house.

A FATTENING PEN FOR A HEN

A most unusual abode for today but common in the 18th century, the fattening pen, where obviously a chicken was kept and treated with ''Tender Loving Care'' unfortunately in preparation for a festive family meal.

Before the use of vitamins a fowl was usually quite old and tough when it finally reached a heavy weight.

I recall 25 and 30 pound turkeys on our Thanksgiving table as a child. They were home-grown on our farm and required many, many hours of roasting to tenderize and to cook thoroughly through. It had taken many months and turkey old age to reach that poundage.

Today, with modern scientific enlightenment a young fowl may quickly reach a plump and tender size. We recognize the differences in the grocery stores with labeling for stewing, roasting and frying graduating from toughest to most tender.

A fattening pen located in the farm-yard at the George Wythe House in Colonial Williamsburg, Virginia.

FEED THE BIRDS

Now that we have our feathered friends residing in a vast array of suitable and very attractive abodes we should give some thought to feeding them.

This is an interesting sampling of some unusual and ornamental feeders.

A bird Diner from Randy Sewell.

A steepled pavilion by Ken Dickinson.

A luxurious thatch from English Thatch.

Some final musings for back porch pondering:

What is the empty nest syndrome?
Why do we speak of feathering our nests?
What is a nest egg?
Is a bird brain really a good label for a person?
Do birds of a feather flock together?
Do bluebirds really bring happiness?
Why do we call someone an old crow?
Why do people parrot others?
Is having bird legs an attribute?
Is nestling cozy and warm?
What is bird's eye maple?
Have you ever seen a midnight bed thrasher?
"It's for the birds", means what?
Why do we call someone "my little Chickadee"?
Do you eat like a bird?
Have you ever had a bird's eye view of something?
What does a goose egg stand for?
Where is the crow's nest located on a sailing ship?
Why do we or don't we put all our eggs in one basket?
Has a little birdie ever told you anything?
Have you heard anyone sing like a nightingale?
Shall we go off on a lark?
What is a "birdie" in the game of golf?
Which came first, the chicken or the egg?
What is your swan song?
What is a darning egg?
Has anyone ever called you "chicken"?
What is an "early bird special?"

Now try and think of some of your own!